FINISHING LINE PRESS

www.finishinglinepress.com

A CAFÉ CALLED ORANGE

poems by

Mark Gordon

Finishing Line Press
Georgetown, Kentucky

A CAFÉ CALLED ORANGE

Publisher: Leah Maines

Editor: Christen Kincaid

Cover Art: Brandon MacLeod

Author Photo: Brandon MacLeod

Cover Design: Brandon MacLeod

Order online: www.finishinglinepress.com

Author inquiries and mail orders:
Finishing Line Press
P. O. Box 1626
Georgetown, Kentucky 40324
U. S. A.

Table of Contents

To Carol

I HEAR A MYSTIC CHANTING NUMBERS

I hear a mystic chanting numbers
      when I arise in the morning
adjust the toaster again
to get that balance
      of burnt to plain
I take my morning walk
    the mystic singing under the tower crane
      something beautiful about wildflowers
numbering the petals
      in fibonacci spirals
         sighing about
the everlasting design
           I hear those sandals
follow me
urging me to observe
       my truest self
    the one that reaches like the birches'
silvery leaves
      toward the sun

ALL OF MORNING

All of morning is a tempting decoy
   to our game
      osprey or seagulls
        (we can't decide)
   that wheel above the reservoir
    that shoal of clouds above the waking
blue, enough to drive
     us mad, swimming in infinity
        far beyond our ken
yet we continue
   to mark the scores
     shoot at distant targets
        knock down the flags
  worried that if we look once more
     at morning unfolding
       we will lose this game
though it be lost anyway
    by and by
        surrendered to the dew wet earth

THIS DAY TOO MUST HAPPEN

"There are days that must happen to you"
        Walt Whitman

This day too must happen
    when I found out a friend lost his wife
        the suddenness
            of an aneurysm
                like a river roaring
                    sweeping her away
                        in the middle of her work
then tears in my eyes
    for his loss
        for something else too
            for the realization that we all depart
            in the middle of something
swept away
    from the home we've known
        the trees, the streets, the memories,
        loved-ones who watch us sail
            on the flood

ONE GIRL GALLOPING

One girl galloping
    around the pond
        seeding the air with energy & laughter
            her young brother asks:
                why is she running?
her wild eyes tell us
    she's running
        to catch the wind
            to tell the trees
                that she's alive
                    ready to embrace this century
                    or any other
we watch, admiring
    how easily
        her legs carry her
            beyond doubt
                (a monster she's not yet met)
she is seeding the air
    with everything we remember
        nights long ago
            running down alleys, reaching
                to touch the moon's hem

KITE FLYING

Sure, it started with the idea
that the wind, this unseen force
would take this thing
we built from newspaper,
branches, mother's old nylons
grab it from our hands
strain at the string
the spool whining
the string cutting our skin
drag it into realms

close to the sun
and somehow
holding tight
we'd go with it
partners of the wind
no more little boys
but more powerful
than teachers, and did we dare say
more daring than our parents

FATHER & SON

Saw a father & son today
walking over hills together
rush of the river
in their talk
butterflies in their glances

drew me back
to childhood days
playing catch with my dad
the baseball coming full tilt
into my catcher's mitt

I wondering
if I had the strength
to hold what was flying at me
to survive the challenge

yet somehow the days unfolded
with the wind hurling
everything it had
and I standing against it
catching

the fire
of that old baseball
in my palm

TUNA

They brought the tuna in
one thousand pounds, hung it
tail to head on the wharf.

We kids looked up in wonder
that something so huge
swam beneath our feet
those shining eyes
those fins that no longer
slapped the waves.

The fishermen called
beckoned for us to come closer
showed us the heart
that seemed to pulse
on the fog-draped wharf
offered us bits of it
to use as bait.

We had no sense
of sadness then, no cringe
of gruesome, just dreamed
of what this special bait
would catch.

Years later that tuna comes back
after lovemaking
or drifting down the highway
on a quiet afternoon
something vast and powerful
something sad
taken from the sea
hanging there, in front of my eyes.

TIDE POOL

I thought I was looking
into a tiny eye of the sea
left there for me
to examine, to learn something
about the universe
something about myself
the link
between large and small
the illusion that I was only
these young bones
a nightmare in the dark.

No, I was the ocean
dressed in a cowboy suit
I was something other
than a leaning fisherman
trying to catch
a spike-finned perch
I was the echo
of a faraway shore
that the waves joined
in their rocking.

I carried this home at night
the ocean in my pocket
thought of it
just before sleep took me.
The ocean had deposited me
in this small cottage
given me this mother
this father
then reminded me
that I was something more.

WILD ROSES

Never since has a scent been as strong
   wild roses in front of the cottage
     the sea's salt breath
      on the petals
       my mother's complexion
        her suntan lotion
& I without knowing it then
   was opening like a rose
    like mother's mouth
      when she said good morning
       like the sea when it revealed
      the shadow of a fish
awareness disclosing
   that there was besides my flesh
   another world
    that asked me to travel it
     with gentleness and caring
to honour it with my eyes
   then much later
   with words
    and with touch

AUNT ADA'S EYES

Aunt Ada always had something grave
about her, around the mouth a pucker,
like a flower torn in its center,
eyes that saw more deeply than others,
avenues she invited me to travel.

I wonder now if she journeyed as I did
on those Sunday mornings in her kitchen,
discovered in my eyes something of herself,
something not found anywhere else,
the warmth of those early morning talks.

Sunlight entered the quiet of the kitchen,
nudged through muslin curtains, mingled
with the aroma of perfume and toast,
though it was years before I realized
how deeply her calm gaze had entered,

how it saved me from the slick light
of hard surfaces, from bravado
that never tired of shouting half truths,
as if the world were a knife blade,
or a fist, not quite made for meditation.

The quiet of the kitchen, a different place
where the week's hardness melted;
I looked into eyes that looked into me,
the two of us spinning on a single need,
to see what vulnerable eyes had hidden.

BLUE WASHCLOTH

Sometimes it is something simple
that lingers for decades,
like a blue washcloth on a sink,
like a shaving bowl and brush,
used by the father each morning,
sometimes the boy watched.

What a miracle it was, the blue
washcloth on the back of his neck,
the brush that flicked the cream,
as strange, if not stranger,
than butterflies in the backyard,
difficult as light to catch.

No, it wasn't the act. It was
something unspoken, between the eyes
that watched and the man who shaved,
something forbidden to words,
as if a boy could choke on them,
a father die, struck down.

For such unspoken words, God
commanded Abraham to take Isaac
to the mountain, to strike with a knife
sharpened on unending light.
Only then did God relent,
sending the ram snagged by its horns.

The boy's fingers trembled
as his gaze rose to his father's chin
its caress so filled with love
he disobeyed the first commandment
making this man of faltering flesh,
                              his god.

CLINIC WAITING ROOM

A baby listens to Humpty Dumpty
on a cellphone
never doubting that someone
who resembles Dad
will put that broken egg
back together

A teenager leans into the wall
dancing with a shadow
her imagination casts:
her date of last Saturday night
now suddenly following the beat

A woman with hesitant English
tries to explain
that she's been waiting for the doctor
far too long, her tired eyes,
her interminable life

I am there too
just as noticeable
as I flip through old poems
on an iPad, the words looking brighter
the poet older, more lined

Although no one
not even her Dad
can put Humpty back together again
the toddler has fallen in love
with that poor broken thing
that waits for its deliverance

BIRTH PASSAGE

My mother never tired of telling me
that I struggled in the birth passage
took at least a day to emerge
all ten pounds, eight ounces
of reluctant flesh

as if I knew the harsh lights
of the delivery room, the loud voices
were only the beginning
a crucible, the first test of how swift
I'd be to face a challenge

how there was no time for meditation
for lollygagging, peering from a bridge
at the catfish below as they wove
their way from the bridge's shadow
into light

no time for counting sailboats
on a summer afternoon
"push, push, push, Mrs. Gordon"
and I came out dome-headed
raw forceps scar on my cheek

bruised enough to remember
somewhere in the vaults of my head
the value of simply breathing
the unremarkable minutes
like a wildflower in a meadow.

SKULLS

Skulls I have held more than once
   up to the light of time passing
     twirled them to see Grandfather
       staring back or grinning Uncle Harry
         no bone of course but skulls nevertheless
         the hard memories that never rot

I looked for a flower to place
   in their eye socket
     found nothing but the stem
     of an old story, how so-and-so
       thought he was becoming an opera star
       but not schizophrenic

No matter how many times
   I planted them in the backyard
     they drifted back when I was shaving
     looked over my shoulder
       made me take a sliver out of my lip.

I expect them now on the windowsill
   when I reach for soap
     know they will never leave me
     no more than my skin

AFTER THE GIFT GIVING

After the gift giving
we wonder what storm
transversed the living room floor
how many pieces of ourselves
are sprinkled there
like sparkling confetti.

I see a bird. Yes, I was a bird once
& finally someone has recognized
that the sky still exists
in my eyes.

She was a horse
thundering across the prairie
in a time now depleted
when she knew the next turn
by the grass's scent.

After gift giving
we hunt through mayhem
for something we don't want
to lose, a nuance
we've discovered this day
that fell from our eyes
before we could snatch it away.

SUMMER'S LESSON

To compensate for her paralyzed arm,
her frozen speech, my grandmother
shook a fist at anyone
she was angry at: her nurse,
my grandfather, my mother or me.

We could never figure out
what the source of her anger was.
Was it the glass of grape juice we brought
too late, when she'd lost all desire
for it? Was it a program

she despised on TV, or was it Fate itself
that had left her in her daughter's
house, in a portion of the living room
that folding doors had designated
as her and grandfather's bedroom?

She showed us how quickly
a weakened vessel could explode
leave a once smiling, content woman
dribbling prune juice from a corner
of a twisted mouth. Each one of us

learned that summer that money,
mansions, and beauty itself
were temporary baubles to keep us
from thinking of that dark storm
that rose on summer evenings

from stillness, found the weakest part
of what we had hitherto considered
inviolable as youth, as the melody
in the throat of the swaying ocean
where sunset planted its crimson path.

HEAD OF THE YEAR

I gaze back to warm September days,
when I walked to the synagogue
with my grandfather, like boys I saw today,
eager and reluctant. Their eyes swivel
to the world, then inward to the pouch
that hides the silken prayer shawl.

Back then no policemen stood guard
seeming embarrassed to look too closely
at the men in skull caps hunched in their task,
the women in knee-high boots, perfumed
to the roots, their laughter full of lipstick,
their capped teeth challenging the sun.

I resist the temptation to say the Lord's
not here, recalling the Lord is everywhere
like one of Ezekiel's whirling wheels
that touches the edge of each human planet.
Its emerald fire wakens dead eyes
to the shimmering elm trees aimed at the sky.

And so another head of the year passes,
my grandfather long since dead.
He died in the middle of his morning walk,
as abruptly as a shriek from the shofar.
His eighty-six-year-old heart folded
in the bright Miami sun, as a plane

high in the sky with a trailing banner
invited one and all to Joe's Oyster Heaven.

LAST NIGHT MY MOTHER ASKED

Last night my mother asked me
if I liked her at all.

Eighty-eight blackbirds,
each for a year of her life, flew
into the sanctum of my ears.

Sixty seven bells, each
for a year of mine, rang
the saddest carillon I could imagine.

But, Mom, I said
you taught me how to knit—
scarves that any comic book hero
would envy, with needles
that clacked like your tongue.

You told me that lightning
was the burning tip of God's cigar,
and thunder the barrels he rolled
down the steps of heaven.

You smelled of suntan lotion, Mom,
when you took me to the beach
and I pretended you were my girlfriend,
saltier than any chunk of spruce gum
I cut from a sea-torn tree.

Do you like me at all? you asked.
Not as a mother but me?

And I wondered how I could divide you
from the woman who took me to movies
when I was four, like trying to cut the

wind in two, or separate you
from the person who told me

I would never be the man
my father was.

Like is not for mothers, Mom.
For mothers is the long tangle
of endearment that runs like a jaguar
through the woods, that occasionally
turns and devours one of its own,
and keeps on striding, as if trying
to outpace its loving shadow.

A LITTLE HOUSE HAS FALLEN

A little house has fallen in my mother's mind.
I wonder if it looks like the garage
beside the raspberry patch she loved
or the cottage out at Queensland
with all the bees visiting the wild roses.
Ah, the smell of wild roses,
so difficult to forget and who would want to?

Something has fallen inside her mind,
this woman who taught me how to dance
jitterbug steps from the forties
that she adapted to rock and roll.
Sometimes I think she is playing a game
just pretending to be mad
as she used to feign to be a witch
for my amusement when I was a kid.

I wonder if the little house has windows
through which she sees another world
one painted with lavender, her favorite colour.
I hope the world she views is not ravaged
by fire. Yes, let it be lavender, like
one of those wildflowers in the park
so tiny I have to bend down to really see
what it is made of. Let it be lavender

as in her bedroom long ago when
I brought her compresses for her forehead
to reduce the pincers of the migraine.
And she said: Close the curtains, dear,
I can't stand the light anymore
it is much too bright and full of knives.
And I pulled the drapes, enclosed her
in those waterfalls of lavender, her house,
her temporary house, for those hours of pain.

WINTER SHAMROCK

Yes, the doc says, the x-ray shows
the lungs are crystal clear, a reef
of perfection, and you go out
like a child once again running
in spring grass as if the Almighty

has cleared you for take off.
And what has the doc given you?—
a few more years of hijinks
mingled with pain. And you think
it must be something more

a chance to turn yourself inside
out, like a shamrock almost dead
from winter dark, that flowers
not just with ordinary petals
but with laughter of the order

of peace on earth. Why else
this invisible jumping up and down
all the way home to your wife
to swing her around with fervour:
love, just love, your blue, blue eyes?

ALLEY WILDFLOWERS

I was torn between picking
the alley wildflowers
yellow and wind-tossed
or just letting them be.

I'd never pick all of them
an anti-communal act
denuding the alley
for everyone else.

But even three
seemed the taking of life
knowing they would
have fewer days
in a vase of water
on the kitchen table.

But I plucked them anyway
to see their gold
reflected in her smile
surviving there in her eyes
far longer than the first frost.

OPHELIA

I've never known an Ophelia.
I've known a Helen, an Elizabeth,
a Rosamine too
but never an Ophelia
with weeds in her hair
her eyes as mad as a stormy sky
but the ladies I've known will do

Now the river's Ophelia
never poured her scent
on my desiring skin
never read me the Song of Songs
on a quiet summer roof
never sculpted a homage
to my privates

And that Ophelia of old
never left a room in my heart
where she sang her songs
for years to come
made me wonder what if
we had built a house
down by the sea together

LOLLING ABOVE THE OCEAN

As we sit in the hodgepodge lunch space
upstairs at Loblaws, with its plastic
tablecloths, its fake wicker chairs,
I look out the giant windows, imagine
that we are lolling above the ocean
in some faraway magic land. The boats

nod on the waves. Someone reaches
for a bottle of champagne. And the sun
burrows into every shadow eagerly.
I realize that the vision is not a wish,
but a picture of what is really going on,
here in this strange place, where meals

are swallowed hurriedly. The ocean
is not miles away, but in the way you turn
your head, in the way I grin at things
you say. The boats are the easy breaths
we take, and the sun is a god above us
who searches for something we possess.

ANTIQUE ROSE

The world rolls over one more time,
tsunami in Japan, the reactors broken,
European banks charred, engulfed
in debt. I watch from the imaginary
safety of my chair, not sure if I should run
as some do, to the country, deep
in the hills, with my cans of sardines.

And then the scent, wafting through
the apartment, of the rose I gave you
for our twenty-first. In no way
will the rose save me, nor will love
but they are enough to inspire—
I open the page of the world again,
view the headlines, know there is news
the journalists have foolishly omitted.

JACOB'S LADDER

The staircase up to the small-town church
they dubbed Jacob's Ladder, though no angels
were ever seen climbing heavenward
entangled in someone's dream, but we
heard it creak on summer nights, perhaps

under the weight of teenagers in love
who felt no guilt or desecration
when their sighs mingled, no ambition
to climb those enticing stairs farther
than the street above, or past the scent

of August pears. Though angels of a sort
did trail their light, fathers whose hair
had turned to snow, mothers who carried
in their aprons a child's nostalgia,
news of their passing, swift or slow,

heard across town. Honoured it became
that rickety ladder that bore generations
to an aging church, and who could say
that angels did not sing on summer nights
with voices as familiar as those steps

that ached in the arches of our feet
that carried us in their equanimity
to all the places we were going?

THE TASTE OF LOVE

Since you asked, friend,
love has no taste.

It is nothing like a fresh loaf of pumpernickel
on a Saturday morning, hot
from the oven
nor is it like spitting watermelon seeds
when we were kids
nor is it a popsicle, a clementine,
a Brando pizza, or a succulent string of figs.

And you certainly can't catch it
throw it into a duffel bag
like contraband ivory tusks.

So you ask, how will you recognize it
when it comes along
when it sallies down the boulevard
like some dish under an umbrella
smelling of eiderdown.

You see, friend, it's more
like the wind.

It catches you
when you least expect it
drags you along
no matter what you are eating
no matter how good it tastes
no matter how firmly your feet are planted.

THREE SPARROWS

When you tell me
that the three sparrows
that you saw on the windowsill
brought tears to your eyes

I am reminded of our journey
why I've taken it with you.
I thrash around for a second
for meaning: deceased relatives

the magnificence of nature
Jung's synchronicity. But then
my mind quiets down. I gaze
into your blue eyes

feel the tenderness you felt
for those tiny birds
that contemplated you
through the kitchen window.

THAT LITTLE CLICK

for Carol

You wave at me far off down an alley.
It knocks me a bit left or right
as though we met yesterday
but it's been a stack of years.

That little click, that something
or other, oh yes, it's still there.
If you try to name it, it flies off,
circles back in a tear.

I think of camping
way back then, fighting off a migraine
before I could hammer tent pegs in
but we unfolded the sky
by and by, fried salami
in a pan.

I think of you visiting me
in rehab, always bringing
those blue eyes
that gripped me from the beginning
as if they knew we'd last:

two waifs like us
off kilter, at times shy,
but something held us
in its palm
as a child cradles a buttercup
for the first time.

IN THAT PLACE

they walk around with bandages
over their eyes

we can see far below
breath curling from chimneys
cars revving up for the day

an old couple sits
in the waiting room with us
her eye covered in Elastoplast
his elbow touching hers
as if he's dreaming of long-ago meadows
how they lay beneath the sunlight
laughter easy then

now her lip swollen & pouting
with a lifetime of trouble.

I stand up again
look out from this 6th story room
to the lake in the distance
covered in smoke and fog
shrouded by winter

glance at the old couple again
and see us in them
our long journey
our bruised mouths

THAT PLACE UP THE RIVER

They come down the river
in a canoe, wave at you,
these people who know the river
as we know cafes in the city.

They wave, mistaking you for a friend
or relative, someone they know
as they walk up the hill
from the river.

You are excited to be accepted like this,
as the sun befriends a meadow.

You ask them how far they've travelled

We've come from way up the river,
they say.

You dream of this at night
that place way up the river
that you know somehow
deep inside, the grazing deer
the caribou moon.

NIGHT TRAIN

Admit it. Something is chasing you.
You hear it in the laughter of the children
in the pool, as if they are embracing
the trees, will never let them go.

You ask yourself: how long ago
did you speak to trees,
how long ago did you reign
along the seashore, master
of the waves?

Let it up. Something is chasing you
like the shadow of a leopard
and you cannot help but admire
the burning green eyes,
the soft pad of the feet
past midnight.

Admit it. Sometimes you feel
like a sack of flesh used up,
its days numbered in wrinkles.

Your wife says: you seemed
not yourself today, more serious
than usual, preoccupied.

Admit it. You are having an affair
with something far off
that sounds like a train at night,
crossing a riven land, its hoot
crying for you to board.

SKIN & WOOD

When I first saw Duchamp's nude
descending a staircase
            I realized that nudes
& staircases would never be the same
one uprooted from her skin
the other losing its hold
on nails & wood
          falling into a netherworld
             with the nude, a blurred place
             that let us contemplate
our skin
our wooden houses
with less delusion for how we saw them
the day before the painting appeared
        & with more respect for the flight
          skin and wood were capable of
            taking us with them
  on this new descent

DALI KNEW A THING OR TWO

Dali knew a thing or two
about clocks hanging twisted
from trees, curled his moustache
at things left half done
    knew that time
        that spiked-faced assassin
        waited to wrap
          unfinished lives
            like gutted fish
                in yesterday's newspaper.

I, too, have tried to outrun
the wind, saying that one more breath
would be enough to turn around
a squandered life
      yet saw such beauty this morning
        in the pink-orange leaves
          of dying autumn
            knew that we all go our way
              having not quite finished
            what we started
& the wings we wanted to grow
have somehow been singed
and some most exquisitely so.

WHITE BIRDS

after Monet's "Cliff Walk at Pourville"

White birds on the sea
a parasol on the shore
I walked there with my mother
and remember it now
not for the thrill of the cliff.

No, not for my tiny hand
in hers, but rather for
the scent of the sea
the salt that always made me feel
like a white bird on the waves.

Then I took flight
when least expected
like Monet's bright flash of light
on a path no one could follow
not even ma mere.

POPPIES

in memory of my grandmother

I could get lost in poppies back then
in Russia in 1890
when I was no older than eight.

It comes back to me
as I stand in front of this Monet
the colour of the poppies
the smell of the fields
the sunlight
on my mother's shoulders.

That was all before 1912
when we were told
terrible things
would happen in Russia,
before the poppy fields turned
into nostalgia, sad memories
of the parents I left behind.

Now I think of that wild day
I ate the seeds
of the spike-boled poppies
by mistake
when I was fourteen
and ran like a horse
through the fields
in an opium fever, laughing.

An old woman now, I let myself
drown in the memory
of that summer,
in the feeling that I, even I,
was once young, carefree
in a field of poppies.

LAGOON GIRL

after Sulamith Wülfing

I have lain here for centuries
preserved by my dreams
some would consider
twisted and dark
like the one last night—

the sea serpent ship
approaching a castle in mist.
I look no older than eleven
as I sprawl among the weeds
of an ancient lagoon

but don't be deceived
I am eons aged and if I didn't
dream these fantasies of mine
I would look quite the crone
furrowed from head to toe.

But you see, this ship
that seems a fright in sail
carries me along
past the nagging aches
of the day. Some say I'll die

just sink to the bottom
of this acrid swamp, but I say
that until the moon falls out
of the sky, I will lie here
musing in its light.

MOTHER WITH A PARASOL

after Monet's "Woman with a Parasol"

When mother strolled with her parasol
she grew as tall as the passing clouds
and I seemed to dwindle
like one of the flowers
she enjoyed bending over
murmuring to it in baby talk
even as she did with me
though I was a sturdy eight-year-old.

I guess I secretly liked her cooing
having never asked her to stop
for who would hear it anyway
out in the fields?

I was her little man when father
was away on business
when I imagined
what it would be like
to be her paramour.
I thought it would resemble
a bee in the centre of a rose
burrowed into its softness.

The wind laughed at me
for all my foolish imaginings.
The clouds gazed down at me
through my mother's parasol.
They seemed to wonder
if I'd ever grow up
or just stand in that field forever
awestruck by her smile.

TWO FIELD HANDS

after Van Gogh's "The Siesta"

As we in the city might dream
of haystacks, the scent
of straw under a teal sky
be transported
from our ordinary selves

to something softer, they hear
the wheels of locomotives
tugging them to Paris
a café near the Eiffel Tower
enmeshed in voices.

The painter stands transfixed
between two worlds:
his brother's art galley
that sells most everything
but his work. Now he has

given himself to forgetfulness
a life of two field hands
how the earth molds them
to itself, the way the sky
kneels down in prayer.

No one, it seems, is content
for long, in the fields,
in the thunder of great cities,
but like a bird in its seasons
seeks out the peace it needs.

A COUNTRY BRIDGE

after Monet's "The Water-Lily Pond"

A bridge always makes me think
that I am leaving one world and entering another
even if both sides contain the same flowers
the exact same scent of countryside
I've known since I was a boy.

So a wooden bridge contains the way we've used
the word, the structure by which
we cross unpredictable waters
even if they appear serene.

I think of that bridge on which a wind-uprooted tree
fell, destroying it, its power to convey us
any longer from what we were
to what we would become, now a heap
of broken cement.

The painter knew the power of this simple
assemblage of wood, knew that he would pass
from lilies, weeds, and grass
to something beyond his ability to imagine

as he waited there for the paint to dry,
for his creation to carry him to the glowing other side.

OLD WORK SONGS

for Alan M

Once in a while
he tells me he's dying
only a few months more wrapped
in this familiar sun
      then he gets out this guitar
          strings as tough as telephone wires
              digs up these tears and struts
               from the Mississippi Delta
                    old work songs pretending to be
                    rock & roll.
I think if this guy's dying
who the hell's living anyway?
      He's down at the mouth of this river
          telling us this is the last song
              he's ever going to play
                 while a single note hangs on
and I swear I'd hear it
as I'm crossing that last washed out road
      I'd sense it ringing in my ear
          crack of a tree tumbled by lightning
              a memory of everyone bearing the load
                 lifting the weight of another day together

WATERCOLOURS

in memory of Barbara King

Knowing that cancer had settled
in her liver, she painted
in watercolours, more ephemeral
than oils, like the cottage she sold
on the island, broken by storms

Once in a while a stalwart tree appeared
like the Arbutus, jutting out
of rock, determined to be seen
one last time, before night
swept in

As she grew closer to those
fragile colours, to the wind blowing
from the everlasting Pacific, light
grew in the greens, the yellows,
and the blues. It was as though she

were turning into a windblown plant
that the Pacific tinted with its waves

A RUSSIAN STUDENT PLAYS THE VIOLIN

From a certain angle, it looks
like a lost world; if you tilt your head
you can smell old aromas
of cabbage soup that grandmother cooked
the sprawling Russia she came from.

In some way you were there
when Stravinsky composed the Rite
when Dostoyevsky walked in the fog
of St. Petersburg, sick of man's sadism,
when ordinary people put on puppet shows

for children. There, never in body,
but in some primeval memory that runs
down the ladder of your spine, walks
like an ache in your instep, there
when your great-grandfather spoke

with the priest in the middle of the night
about messiahs coming and going. There
when the priest sent the townspeople
out with staves to wave off Cossacks
on their snorting horses, thirsty for the blood

of Jews. There with her, when she played
the violin in Minsk, as she plays it now,
tucked so tenderly under her chin
no lover could ever usurp. There
with her in another life, another body,

walking with her in the sensual air, where
all the trees were violins, and you a juggler,
or a painter, or just a sad, shivering horse
that she ran her hands over, there
in a lost world you somehow believe in
as much as anything you have since found.

A CAFÉ CALLED ORANGE

Sitting in this café called Orange
(named perhaps for the colour
of its exterior brick)
it seems that the people walking
in the snow, move
in a reverie, most of them
hurrying to work or school.

I suppose it is the vantage point,
lounging here, a warm latte
in my hand, that makes me feel
that I am somehow real,
no longer bound to rushing,
no job to hurl myself toward.

And I suspect when they
glance through the veil of snow
seeing me through the window
that I appear the dreamer,
distant, aloof, no pressing need
like theirs. So we are reflections
of each other's fancy.

Sitting in the café called Orange
I wonder if the one who named it
was thinking of the phantoms
in the snow, or the lone dreamer
lolling by the window, a cup
to his lip, the café's peculiar name
giving contour to the morning.

MOTH

One could do worse than bird watching
on this deck, just reclining
in a cup of sun
        one could be out
          slitting the throat of a stranger
for money
for gang fame
for a lover's sigh
        one could be straining on a river
          for the sake of a prize
            at the next rowers' meet
instead of watching
this woodpecker
tap on the wooden rail
of the deck
        this blue-jay spread its wings
          like a fox-trot dancer
            catching the first light
              of 5 a.m.
                this chickadee
                  turn itself upside-down
                    to glean the last pellet
                      of birdseed from the feeder
one could be doing worse
by hunting for that dead moth
that fell behind the sofa
its wings singed
        asking yourself why
          why you must find this tiny emblem
            of our mortality

THE EGO'S EMBRACE

It's hard to avoid the embrace
of the Ego; it's a charismatic, sexless thing
that steps in when you are praying
or simply taking a walk
offers you heady opportunities
like world power, a trophy wife
or a brand-new Ferrari.

You say "let go of my hair,
don't pull like that,
I am just taking a stroll in the woods
reciting Psalm 23
watching the way the veins
of this leaf are opening
leading me to a deeper understanding."

But the Ego, as always,
has a different idea of pleasure
fogging your glasses with excitement
putting you on stilts
that no one else owns
saying you will see over mountains.

It leaves you just as suddenly
with no more eyes to see
how you and this leaf are one
both breathing the light of galaxies
both unfolding
season after season
arriving at a depth of your own.

STREET OF HOUSES

There is a street of houses
that wakes in me the desire
to wrap a house around me
like an old familiar coat.

I will become that man
who is sitting on the steps
of his house, its lattice work
like an angel who comforts.

I will take the house with me
on all my departures, wear it
on my return, a bodyguard
when nights are dark, a lover

in the morning. I will forget
that I have never possessed
a house, as my father did,
feign that trees have grown

through my blood, generation
after generation, pretend
that I have not broken with
the lineage of ownership

and let the image of a house
lift me, if only for the minutes
I drive down the street, sighing
in the warmth of my body.

OUTCASTS

Ever since I was a kid
it was the outcast
I was attracted to, someone
who didn't quite fit in
                    the girl who leaned to one side
                        as she walked, pensive
                            as a falling leaf, the guy
                                who came from the country
                                    claiming to know
all the symphonies the wind played.
                        Schooling & age
                            have not changed me
                                have only confirmed in me
                                    a love of the eccentric
a woman as shy as a hummingbird
a man who lies on his back
contemplating the clouds
telling me how much he loved his mother
back then in that small town
                        and over the years I've come to realize
                            that they were glimpses of myself
                                the kid who hated school
                                    the boring routines of camp
but loved to stand on a bridge alone
watch the catfish swimming
in purplish grey waters
between the beams of shadow and light

TOWER OF WINDS

It gives me a shiver
to picture that old Greek weathervane
in the Tower of Winds
the tower of what?
Winds. Winds, like the god Triton.
        Just try to picture
            that tower in ancient Greece
                spinning north, south, east
then imagine
yourself up there
with the sea wind
coming off the Mediterranean
& you suddenly being able to hear
the voices of the gods
           telling you that these blasts
              can scatter you in a blink
                to anywhere in the universe
                  or if today they happen to be kind
                    gather you in their mercy
                      to a ride with Aphrodite
high above the bickering earth
in her swan-drawn chariot.

THE KIND OF DAY

The kind of day
when you don't get up too fast
let the rain outside
slap the pavement
        remind you of days long past
           the swaying liners at port
              their ropes that knocked
                 at morning softly
ships that you saw coming & going
taking for granted your life
by the sea, accepting
the scent of salt as a right
        not realizing how it ferried you
         past the harbour narrows
        to continents that once
          were molded to yours.
Only years later inland
would you see
what you grew up with:
        fog that carried another misty day
        to your doorstep, you
       who wore it
         like an old familiar coat.

IN TIMES LIKE THESE

In times like these
there is a boat
that we might sail
past the melting ice
the cries of war

I will not utter
its name, although
people whisper it
daily, hands clasped,
on their knees

I will simply jump
aboard, take my
songs, my tendency
to talk to trees
in times like these

INSOMNIAC'S PRAYER

Sleep catches you
when you are tired enough
imprint of a bed on your back
nothing to do
but close your eyes
     a hypnotist's gold watch
         swings you on your head's stem
          the mind's timepiece
when you are tired
of roaming all night long
the avenue of your imaginings
as you shoot what you think you want
with a BB gun at the fair
         an endless row of ducks
          to win something to hug
           even to love
             that you throw out dust laden
the following year
then utter the insomniac's prayer
"I surrender every desire
to this one half hour of sleep"
         & only the clock when you awake
          reveals that sleep caught you
           in that millisecond between lusts
like a tiny death
to the aches of the world
to its seizures of yearning

LYING ON A COT ALONE

Sometimes you cannot help but hear.
They walk up and down the hallways
talking of death. You are in a bundle,
a fragile filter to the hints of the end.

These are solemn words, holy words,
for they are free of the desire for gain,
enter all like the simplicity of night,
bite to the root. And you lie seized

by an odd craving not to move.
Death, this new potion they feed you,
together with vitamins and drips,
and tell you it will make you stronger.

You sip and all the melodious songs
of your life crack in your throat
like outcast crows, and you never want
to live without death again, so clean

it makes you feel, so honest,
like Van Gogh standing in a field
with a cold revolver to his temple
searching for the ultimate shade of blue.

THEN CAME SOME BUDDHISTS

First came the Black nurse
who placed her hand on my leg
read me psalm 91,
commanded the evil spirits to leave
in the name of Jesus,
I hummed along
as she sang *Amazing Grace*.

Then came the Priest
who placed my quivering hand
on a black Bible,
whispering something in Latin
that I struggled to decipher,
from what I had learned in grade nine.

Then came the Rabbi
who asked if I wanted kosher food,
promised to mention my name
at the next gathering of the tribes,
then looked into my eyes,
as if he were contemplating the pools
of Ein Gedi.

Then came some Buddhists
who tinkled their bells,
who never stopped grinning,
who promised to carry me like a wisp
of smoke across the great divide.

Then came a Nurse
who hugged me at midnight
on New Year's eve
and told me miracles were possible.

Then came my wife
with some figs I had requested.
And I looked into her eyes,

seeing how cold and deep
was the great divide
that would separate me from her.

Then came Death
braying like a donkey
with rotten teeth.

I rode him to Jerusalem like a fool,
waving my fronds of palm,
speaking in a thousand tongues,
as the angels applauded.

Then came reprieve like a brash March wind.

It took hot spikes of rickety breathing
to gather the remnants of prayer,
squeeze them into a toiletry bag
along with my toothbrush,
making sure not a shred dropped out
as I pushed my way
through the hospital's revolving door.

HANDS

With age the veins in the hands
grow thicker.
        Some would hide their hands
behind a newspaper
under a desk.

Gaze, however, at all the years
to produce those hands
the writing in grade one
to make the "L" lean
the "W"
to sail on a pond.

The snapping of the fingers
in teenage years
to attract a girl
but never the love
you wanted.

The pressure on those hands
in youth as you caught
chickens by the neck
at midnight
to prove you were almost
a man.

It took years and years
to create those swollen rivers
each vein with a story
as sad as a job
that never worked out,
fixing TVs in a factory,
lugging mail from door to door
dreams that shattered
in sunlight.
        Now let your hands flutter
for the world to see

to recognize itself
in the way you wave
or fold them into a house
of prayer.

PIGEON SESTINA

Though he couldn't read he kept pigeons,
housed them in the backyard in a shed,
had a woman older than himself,
a pinch-faced, lonely-eyed, loving woman
who rode him like a pony during the night,
she was his wee rabbit, his great delight.

In all things that breathed he took delight,
monkeys, goldfish, people and pigeons,
people that is who didn't disturb the night,
like wolves among the pigeons in the shed,
people with the heart and mind of his woman
who embraced pulsing critters like himself.

For these he would make a road of himself
for them to travel, to revel and delight,
would give them his rabbits and his woman,
if they didn't judge him but cooed like pigeons
perched in the topmost rafters of his shed,
friends of his frailty in the darkest night.

But if they came roving in the bloody night
intent on mocking his woman or himself,
he would take them out to the lonely shed,
show them anything but what you'd call delight
until screams flew up among the pigeons,
and they said sorry and cried like a woman.

He wondered why man never learned from woman
the tenderness that she showed in the night,
but feasted on death and the blood of pigeons,
no love for anyone, not even himself,
never looking at the moon for his simple delight,
never cooing to pigeons in a creaky shed.

All this he would think of in his shed,
when no one was there, not even his woman,

when he looked inward for his one delight
saw what his soul hid in the heaving night,
how his comfort now was only himself,
and the fluttery cooing of his dozing pigeons.

He looked at the delights that all the years shed,
tried to see them clearly: woman and pigeons
gone into the night, and at last, himself.

TIRED OF EATING

Tired of eating? I know that feeling.
Never thought I'd say it.
How long must you have travelled
down what gouged roads
to admit it?

The wheat fields await your tongue,
the tired beasts in the pastures
look untrustingly at your teeth.
You eye the mountain of French Fries
you masticate each year.
No wonder you get those pains,
then speculate on which organ
is unraveling.

Don't fret about not wanting to ingest
another henhouse worth of eggs.
This feeling, I believe,
is earned with age:
We have eaten our way
halfway around the world
have tasted sex, ambition, lies
isn't natural to take a rest?
Lay down our chopsticks & our knives

ALLEY CATS

I saw him this morning, spoon
in hand, as he came back from feeding
the alley cats, his trousers frayed.

I've seen him for years, walking
through the alley, looking for the cats
that hide between the garage
and overgrown backyards.

I've never seen him in conversation
with anyone, but I imagine the dialogues
he has with the cats, intense
communications about what it is like
not to have a home, to be allocated
by fate to the dark places
between cement and high grasses.

THE GREAT SADNESS

Not a personal sadness, more like the sound
of cars on a rainy day
as they slap their rhythms on pavement
a grief for the universe
that travels from Jupiter's bulk
to a dying tulip on the kitchen table.

In this gloominess, the tears are mixed
with a meadow's tranquility
the knowledge that I am part of a sorrow
that is much larger than myself
a lament that encompasses
the Sahara with every hissing snake

each scorpion. The oceans invade me
with their tears, the mountains sigh
as if they are children who
want to be hugged, the sun drops a tear
that becomes a comet's tail,
and I ride this melancholy with no idea

where it ends. I think of the fireball
that started it all, sent the planets
spinning in ever wider circles
and how like an accordion it will all
fold in on itself, while making
the sweetest music. Oh sadness

what is your name? Where are you
bearing us? The games we played
are turning to rust, like that old
Meccano set when I was seven
its motors too tired to turn, its wheels
in a dump somewhere serenely still.

Yet amidst all this infinite woe
I find that I'm laughing more than ever

at jokes I make up, at what my friends
have to say. It comes upon me
in waves, like ocean breakers,
where I first learned to swim in salt.

CONTEMPLAING LIGHT

The light on that pond is broken
by brackish water, weeds,
the shadow of cranes
that peer for fish,
a city pond in the middle
of a golf course, where the light
is complicated
by golf balls going brown
in its embrace, by
the quick flight of minnows
and the stodgy meanderings
of gold fish. Since they are red
I have no idea why they
are called gold. But light
has a way of tricking us, putting
inaccurate words in our mouth.

I have sometimes stood there
in the dreamy light of dusk
just to imagine
what it would be like
to be a gold fish in a pond,
or for that matter, a crane.
Nobody there but me
leaning on the last question
of the day, before the horn blows,
clearing us dreamers away.

THAT SLOW GAZE

A squirrel slithers across a vine-covered wire,
playing a game with me from above,
as its eyes ignite, pretends
to be afraid, knows
it cannot fall.

A tiny sparrow hunts for breadcrumbs
in an alley behind the bagel shop.
And the scent of spring is in the air
that takes me back to Macdonald Street,
that smell, hard to name, like
slate by the ocean, like cabbage weeds
in the backyard, like something
in the black earth, as I watch
the milk truck's horse clop, clop,
up the pot-holed dirt street,
in some lost year of the forties.

They say when you are young
time unwinds slowly, like
string being eaten from a spool
on a day the kite hardly tugs,
and then when you are old
time slows down again,
as if the street's come back
with all its smells,
and I look up to see this squirrel
as I would back then.

I grin, just grin at nothing,
the gift of that slow gaze
in my eyes once more.

TONIGHT THE SKY IS ROSEBUSHES

Tonight the sky is rosebushes
and blue pinafores for as far as
I can see east to west
and all I want to do is stand here
swiveling my neck.

I keep catching sight of something
in the sky, a feeling, a colour, that is
more inviting than before.
It unfolds above me, casual
as my pulse.

I have made my way past construction
you perhaps have been in a war
or just the daily battle
with depression that looks like
mortar from the 19th century.

We gaze at what the sky
has painted. It's the texture
that gets me. It doesn't seem quite real
this sky that makes you stop
your walking, cease your thinking.

We stand here not ever wanting
to move. For you know
that no matter what city you'd run to
what book you'd read, it
would never get better than this.

ACKNOWLEDGEMENTS

I would like to thank Canadian poet, Di Brandt, who edited this collection. Her many insights and suggestions helped improve individual poems and the collection as a whole.

Over decades, Charlie Sise, poet, novelist, and friend, read hundreds of my poems, making suggestions that made me a better writer. For this I am grateful.

I would like to thank my wife, Carol. I would often ask her which line sounded better of two, if a stanza was really necessary, and she, more often than not, made an acute suggestion.

Members of the poetry community on Twitter have continued to inspire me in the last few years with their comments on my poems and with their own poetry. I am grateful to them.

Many thanks to my nephew, Brandon MacLeod, for his excellent cover design.

I would like to thank the following journals that published poems which appear in this collection: *VerseWrights, Illuminations, Canadian Jewish News, Quiddity International Literary Journal, Linden Avenue Literary Journal, Roanoke Review, Phantasmagoria, California Quarterly, RiverSedge, Abstract Magazine: Contemporary Expressions, Tilde, A Literary Journal.*

The last thing on **Mark Gordon**'s mind when he entered the first year at McGill University when he was sixteen was an interest in writing poetry and an interest in literature in general. Since he had just moved with his family from Halifax and knew nobody in Montreal, he joined a fraternity. Besides, he thought it was the "normal" thing to do.

His non-existent relationship to literature changed two years later when he travelled to Tucson, Arizona to do summer studies in sociology and anthropology at the University of Arizona. Somehow, during those hot and arid days, between playing golf on concrete-hard courses, riding a scooter around town, and ostensibly studying, he began to read novels by Steinbeck and poetry by E. E. Cummings. Both of these writers knew how to make language sing and he was immediately enthralled. His previous, childhood reading was the Hardy Boys' mysteries and comic books. What was this spell, he wondered, that these two authors were unexpectedly weaving around his mind?

When he returned to McGill in the fall, he met up with a band of young, student poets who had studied in high school under the tutorship of the up-and-coming Canadian poet, Irving Layton. He read Layton of course, and Louis Dudek, who was one of his professors, and a host of international poets since they were now on courses he had chosen. A love of language as wide as the St. Lawrence River was opening inside him. Dostoyevsky, Rimbaud, Flaubert, T. S. Eliot, Dylan Thomas. It went on and on and included real, live poems being written by Irving Layton's disciples. He wrote his first-ever poem, which started with these auspicious lines, "the sun broke like an egg/over the tailfins of cars."

Over the years that followed, he hopscotched from writing novels to writing poetry, each capturing his time and attention for a season. He was told that his novels were poetic, and his poetry was story-like. It took him much longer to find his voice as a poet than it did as a novelist. He began to understand that the poem was a unit of language, unified by the music of words and the cohesion of meaning. He discovered that he would sometimes let an idea break down the music or the music waylay an idea, and neither was good for the poem.

He learned too that writing is a process. Each poem is an unrepeatable and unique event that a particular time and mood produces. Just as each snowflake is one of a kind, its pattern dictated by temperature, wind, geography and hundreds of other variables, so is the poem. No wonder poets face the blank page with trepidation, utter a silent prayer, and press into their pen or keyboard, not knowing quite where this day's foray will take them.

Gordon hopes that this little volume of poetry will accompany the reader through some of the bends, twists, and exciting leaps he has taken on the journey.

CPSIA information can be obtained
at www.ICGtesting.com
Printed in the USA
BVHW071339070223
658043BV00007B/214